Popcorn

Rivers

Ruth Thomson

WAYLAND

Explore the world with **Popcorn** - your complete first non-fiction library.

Look out for more titles in the Popcorn range. All books have the same format of simple text and striking images. Text is carefully matched to the pictures to help readers to identify and understand key vocabulary.
www.waylandbooks.co.uk/popcorn

Published in 2013 by Wayland
Copyright © Wayland

Wayland
Hachette Children's Books
338 Euston Road
London NW1 3BH

Wayland Australia
Level 17/207 Kent Street
Sydney NSW 2000

Produced for Wayland by
White-Thomson Publishing Ltd
www.wtpub.co.uk
+44 (0)843 208 7460

Editor: Steve White-Thomson
Designer: Amy Sparks
Picture researcher: Ruth Thomson/Steve White-Thomson
Series consultant: Kate Ruttle
Design concept: Paul Cherrill

British Library Cataloguing in Publication Data
Thomson, Ruth, 1949-
 Rivers. -- (Geography corner)(Popcorn)
 1. Rivers--Juvenile literature.
 I. Title II. Series
 910.9'1693-dc22

ISBN: 978 0 7502 7201 8

Wayland is a division of Hachette Children's Books,
an Hachette UK company.
www.hachette.co.uk

Printed and bound in China

Picture Credits: **Corbis**: NASA 15; **Dreamstime**: Emjaysea 12, Mangroove 8, Martinmark 7, McPics 19, Salez 11; **iStock**: Knaupe (cover); **Shutterstock**: akva 4–5, Andy Z. 21, Aperture Untamed 17, Tom Cummins 7, Chris Fourie 14, Iain Frazer 13, Tatiana Grozetskaya 9, Jason Kasumovic 1/16, Simon Krzic 2/10, leolintang 18; **Neil Thomson** 23; **WTPix**: 6, 20.

Every effort has been made to clear copyright. Should there be any inadvertent omission, please apply to the publisher for rectification.

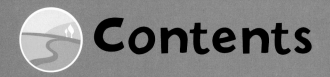 # Contents

What is a river?

A river is a large stream of water that flows downhill over land to the sea. Its sides are called banks. The bottom is the river bed.

The water in rivers is fresh, not salty like the sea.

Rivers slowly wear away
the rocky land. They cut
valleys between hills.
This takes millions of years.

The Colorado River cut through many rock layers to create the Grand Canyon.

Rivers of the world

Some rivers, such as the Nile, Amazon and Congo, are very long. They start in the hills in one country and pass through several others before they reach the sea.

Rivers are often a natural boundary, separating one country from another.

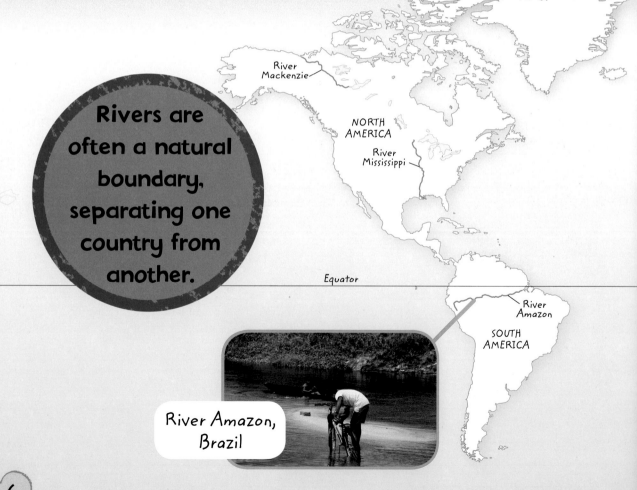

River Mackenzie

NORTH AMERICA

River Mississippi

Equator

River Amazon

SOUTH AMERICA

River Amazon, Brazil

Long ago, towns were built on rivers, because people needed nearby water for drinking, washing and cooking. Traders travelled by boat between towns to buy and sell goods.

This map shows the main rivers in each continent.

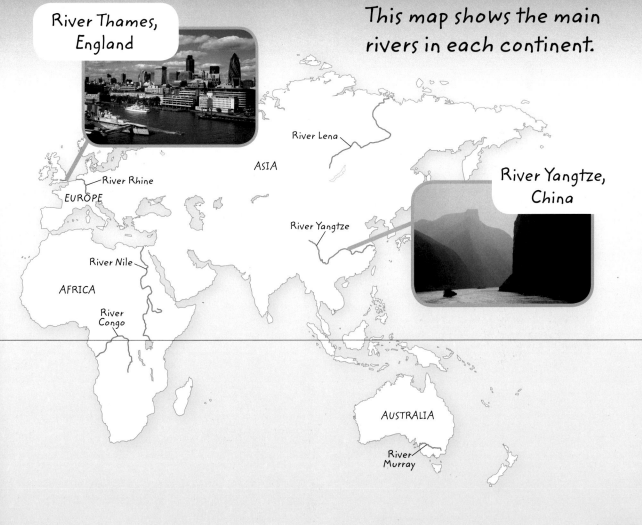

River Thames, England

River Yangtze, China

River Lena

ASIA

River Rhine

EUROPE

River Yangtze

River Nile

AFRICA

River Congo

AUSTRALIA

River Murray

A river's source

Most rivers start high up in hills
or mountains. The place where
a river starts is called its source.
When rain falls or snow melts,
the water trickles downhill.

Mountain water is
always very cold.

The trickles join to form clear, shallow streams. The water rushes down steep hillsides and loosens rocks, stones and soil. These are carried downstream.

Stones knock together and turn slowly into gravel and sand. Soil turns to mud.

Plants cannot take root in rushing streams.

Rapids and waterfalls

Fast-flowing streams swirl round jagged rocks. These are called rapids.

People find it exciting to steer rafts though dangerous rapids.

Streams join together to form a wider, deeper river. Sometimes, this drops over the edge of a rocky cliff. This is called a waterfall.

Waterfalls make a huge spray of water.

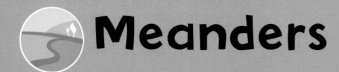

Meanders

As the land becomes flatter, rivers slow down. They wind their way more calmly in giant loops called meanders.

Meanders change the shape of the countryside.

Rivers always find the easiest route. They never flow in a straight line.

Water flows faster on the outside bend of a meander. It washes away sand and soil. Some of this drops on to the inside bend. The meander slowly grows larger.

The wearing away of the river banks is called erosion.

Estuaries and deltas

A river widens into an estuary as it nears the sea. It slows down even more. It drops the gravel, sand and mud it has been carrying.

Birds flock to estuaries. There is plenty of food for them here.

Fresh water mixes with salty water when a river meets the sea.

Sometimes there is so much sand and mud that it blocks a river. The water splits into a fan of side streams and muddy ground called a delta.

delta

Mediterranean Sea

River Nile

EGYPT

Red Sea

This is the delta of the River Nile, seen from space.

River wildlife

Some animals have special features for living in water. Otters, beavers and capybaras have waterproof fur and webbed paws that are like paddles.

Beavers cut down trees with their strong teeth and build dams across streams.

Hippos, frogs and crocodiles have eyes and nostrils near the top of their heads. They can still see and breathe with their bodies underwater.

Hippos keep their bodies underwater all day to keep cool in the hot African sun.

 # Floods

Sometimes heavy rain or melted
snow fills a river too quickly.
The river overflows onto the land.

The rush of floodwater can spill
into streets and houses.

Some rivers flood around the same time every year. When floodwater goes down, it leaves behind fertile soil for growing crops.

Farmers plant rice in flooded fields.

Flood protection

In places that often flood, people build homes on stilts so floodwater cannot reach them. They may also build high walls of earth for protection.

This river can rise 14 metres, so houses on high banks still need stilts.

In some countries, people have built dams to control floodwater. A reservoir behind the dam stores extra water. A constant flow is let out all year round.

Dams are curved so they do not break from the weight of the water.

The force of water flowing from dams can provide electricity.

A river at a glance

A river starts at its source and ends at the sea.

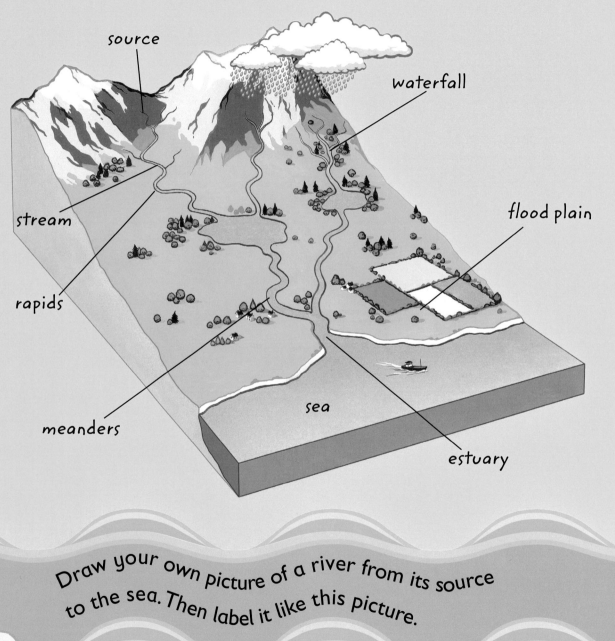

source

waterfall

stream

flood plain

rapids

meanders

sea

estuary

Draw your own picture of a river from its source to the sea. Then label it like this picture.

Make a model raft

1. Take the labels off the bottles. Stand them side by side.

hole

2. Cut a piece of card which is larger than the bottles. Paint it. Get an adult to make a hole in the middle of the card.

3. Cut a card sail. Glue it to the stick.

4. Glue the bottles under the card deck.

5. Push the stick into the card deck to add the sail.

Try floating your raft on some water.

23

Glossary

boundary a line that divides a place from the place next to it

dam a wall across a river that holds water back

estuary the widest part of a river, where it meets the sea

fertile good for growing crops

flood a lot of water covering land that is usually dry

meander a bend in a river flowing over flat land

rapids the parts of a river where water flows quickly around rocks

reservoir a lake made by humans, where water is collected and stored

stilts tall poles that carry the weight of a house near a river

webbed webbed feet have skin joining the toes together

Index